curiousabout
FAIRIES

BY GINA KAMMER

AMICUS

What are you

curious about?

CHAPTER THREE

Finding Fairies
PAGE
16

Curious About is published
by Amicus
P.O. Box 227
Mankato, MN 56002
www.amicuspublishing.us

Editor: Rebecca Glaser
Series Designer: Kathleen Petelinsek
Book Designer: Catherine Berthiaume
Photo Researchers: Bridget Prehn and Omay Ayres

Library of Congress Cataloging-in-Publication Data
Names: Kammer, Gina, author. Title: Curious about fairies / by
Gina Kammer. Description: Mankato, MN : Amicus, 2023. |
Series: Curious about mythical creatures | Includes bibliographical
references and index. | Audience: Ages 6–9 | Audience: Grades
2–3 | Summary: "Survey the legends and folklore about fairy
appearance, behavior, and homes in a fun question-and-answer
format that reinforces inquiry-based learning for early elementary-
age readers. A Stay Curious! Learn More feature models research
skills and doubles as a mini media literacy lesson. Includes simple
infographics, glossary, and index"– Provided by publisher.
Identifiers: LCCN 2020001131 (print) | LCCN 2020001132
(ebook) | ISBN 9781645491279 (library binding) | ISBN
9781681526942 (paperback) | ISBN 9781645491699 (pdf)
Subjects: LCSH: Fairies–Juvenile literature. Classification: LCC
GR549 .K36 2021 (print) | LCC GR549 (ebook) | DDC
398.45–dc23
LC record available at https://lccn.loc.gov/2020001131
LC ebook record available at https://lccn.loc.gov/2020001132

Photos © Shutterstock / Atelier Sommerland Cover, 1, 8–9, 16;
Alamy / Science History Images 4–5; Arthur Spiderwick's Field
Guide / Tony DiTerlizzi & Holly Black 7 (brownie); Shutterstock
/ Algol 7 (pixie); Dreamstime / Linda Bucklin 7 (leprechaun);
Shutterstock / AJMILTON 7 (elf); Shutterstock / Elle Arden Images
10; Alamy / Pictures Now 11; Alamy / Charles Walker Collection
13; iStock / Keith Lance 15 (top); Shutterstock / Dobryanska
Olga 15 (foxglove); iStock / Richard Griffin (hawthorn trees);
Shutterstock / krolya25 (groundsel); Shutterstock / Aleksandr
Pobedimskiy 15 (iron); iStock / AntiMartina 15 (yarrow); iStock
/ scisettialfio 15 (St. John's wort); Shutterstock / Miriam Doerr
Martin Frommherz 17; Manchester Evening News / John Hyatt
18; Shutterstock / Ironika 19; Shutterstock / Vera Petruk 20–21;
FreeSVG / OpenClipart 22–23; pngset / Harley100 22–23

Are fairies real?

Fairy stories go back more than 1,000 years. In **legends**, fairies come in all shapes and sizes. Even leprechauns were thought of as fairies! Some say fairies are gods or were once angels. But no one has hard **proof** they are real.

In some stories, fairies are no bigger than butterflies.

What do fairies look like?

Fairies are said to look like tiny people. Pixies may only be 3 inches (7.6 cm) tall! Elves can be the size of a child or an adult. Fairies are known to change size, too! Tall or tiny, most fairies are beautiful. Today, you usually see fairies with wings. Long ago, fairies didn't have wings.

BROWNIE

PIXIE

LEPRECHAUN

WILL-O'-THE-WISP

ELF

What magic powers do fairies have?

Art often shows fairies with pointed ears.

Fairies are bursting with magic. They fly or move so fast they are hard to see. They can also change their size and shape. Fairies are known to cast **blessings** or **curses**. Earth fairies help plants grow. Will-o'-the-wisps have a magical glow.

CHAPTER TWO

How long do fairies live?

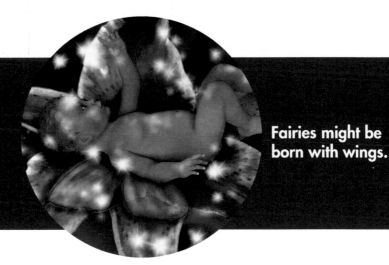

Fairies might be born with wings.

Fairies live a lot longer than people. In one story, fairies are born when babies laugh. Fairies grow like humans do. In the country of Ireland, legends say fairies live forever!

Art often shows fairies getting
along with forest creatures.

What do fairies like to do?

Fairies like to party! For each season, they have big feasts. The summer party is their favorite. Parties have music and dancing. Fairies play beautiful music. For fun, fairies play tricks on people. Pixies often trick people into getting lost.

Fairies weave a magic cloak as they dance.

Are fairies friendly?

Fairies can be both evil and nice. They change their minds a lot. Mostly, they just make **mischief**. But they can be evil to mean people. Fairies don't like people who hurt plants. They do love gifts. They leave gifts for nice people, too.

A drawing of a mean fairy stealing a bird's egg.

FAIRY LIKES AND DISLIKES

foxglove

yarrow

Hawthorn trees

groundsel

iron

Saint-John's-wort

ATTRACTS FAIRIES

KEEPS FAIRIES AWAY

Where do fairies live?

Art shows fairy homes made from mushrooms.

According to legend, fairies live in fairyland!
Fairyland is hidden. It might be under the ground.
Some people believe fairy rings bring you to
fairyland. Fairy rings are circles of mushrooms in
the grass. Legends say to step inside to see fairies.

Fairy rings come in many sizes. The largest one
ever found was about 2,000 feet (610 m) wide.

A professor claims to have photographed these fairies.

Has anyone seen a fairy?

Hundreds of people say they have seen fairies. Have you seen leaves spinning in the wind? Some people believe that means fairies are there. One woman said she saw one when she got lost. The fairy helped her find the right way. Another man saw dozens of fairies in his shop.

Some fairies use magic to make flowers grow.

Some people make fairy houses as decorations.

How could I see a fairy?

Remember, there is no proof they exist. In stories, children are more likely than adults to see fairies. But fairies don't like to be talked about. So don't say the word fairy. Call them something nice, such as "good people." Leave them gifts. Who knows what you'll find?

ASK MORE QUESTIONS

Where can I find an old fairy story?

What really are fairy rings?

Try a BIG QUESTION: How has science changed ideas about fairies?

SEARCH FOR ANSWERS

Search the library catalog or the Internet.
A librarian, teacher, or parent can help you.

Using Keywords
Find the looking glass

Keywords are the most important words in your question.

?

If you want to know about:

- old fairy stories, type: FAIRY LEGENDS

- what fairy rings are, type: FAIRY RINGS

FIND GOOD SOURCES

Are the sources reliable?

Some sources are better than others. An adult can help you. Here are some good, safe sources.

Books

Fairies
by Melissa Gish, 2022.

Fairies
by Suma Subramaniam, 2022.

Internet Sites

Classical Kids Storytime: An Irish Folk Tale

https://www.classicalmpr.org/story/2019/03/05/classical-kids-storytime-irish-folk-tale-nora-fairy-queen

MPR is public radio in Minnesota. It has news and information on many topics.

SciShow: Fairy Rings

https://sharemylesson.com/teaching-resource/fairy-rings-252542

SciShow creates videos about science. Share My Lesson is an educational resource for teachers.

Every effort has been made to ensure that these websites are appropriate for children. However, because of the nature of the Internet, it is impossible to guarantee that these sites will remain active indefinitely or that their contents will not be altered.

SHARE AND TAKE ACTION

Protect nature.
Plant flowers that fairies would like.

Find two or more pictures of fairies.
Compare how they look alike or different.

Draw what you think a fairy would look like.
Show it to your family or friends and tell them why you chose to draw it that way.

GLOSSARY

blessing Something that is helpful or brings happiness.

curse Magical words that cause trouble or bring bad luck.

legend A story from the past that may or may not be true but cannot be checked.

mischief Annoying behavior that causes trouble without hurting.

proof Evidence of something.

INDEX

About the Author

Gina Kammer grew up writing and illustrating her own stories. Now she edits children's books and writes for all ages. She likes to read fantasy and medieval literature. She also enjoys traveling, oil painting, archery, and snuggling her grumpy bunny. She lives in Minnesota.